Levitations

by

Pamela Martin

Levitations
Copyright 2007 by Pamela Gowan

All rights reserved under International and Pan-American copyright conventions. No part of this book may be reproduced, stored in a retrieval system or transmitted in any form, electronic, mechanical, or by any other means, without written permission of the author.

International Standard Book Number: 978-0-615-26491-2

Illustrated by Kathleen Hardy.

Table of Contents

Part I

The Cat-and-Mouse Dichotomy 9
Trying Times 9
Labor Day 9
Anatomy of a Teenager 10
Justin Time 11
B.C. (Birth Canal) 11
Acrophobia...11
Adeste Fideles 12
The Persistence of Memory 12
When History Repeats Itself 12
"La Dolce Vita"...13
Mommy, Dearest...13
Murder, She Wrote 13
Word Power...14
Future Perfect..14
The Elixir of Life 14
Aphrodite 15
A Sober Thought 16
"Placentam edeant!"...16
Keynesian Economics...16
No Pain, No Gain..17
 "Et in Arcadia Ego" 17
A Genteel Sufficiency 17
Heart Strings 18
A Perfect Stranger 18
A Boston Brahmin...18
Discretion is the Better Part of Valor 19
A Veteran of Love 19
An Honest Man 19
Levitations..20
Gender Bias..21
Racial Bias 21
Unbiased 21
"Honest Graft" 22
Strange Bedfellows 22
What's in a Name?..22
Caught in the Crosshairs 23
The Smoking Gun 23
"Eye Popping Good"...23

Part II

Sun to Sun	27
The Hunting Party	27
The Antipode of Heaven	27
Catnip	28
Ambrose Bierce	28
Fantasy Island	28
Deaf Ears	29
Genetic Determinism	29
Proceed at Your Own Peril	29
Plunder	30
Wordplay	31
Cognitive Dissonance	31
Smoke Screen	31
Screw the Middleman	32
Black Death	32
Que sera, sera!	32
Heat Wave	33
A Half Truth	33
Greco-Roman Decadence	33
A Police Intervention	34
"A Wanton Disregard"	34
Eternity	34
Sanctuary	35
Disillusionment	36
Greek Freak	36
Spiritual Cremation	36
Triage	37
Voyeurism	37
Bibliomania	37
Glasnost	38
V-J Day	38
"Fraternite"	38
Flotsam and Jetsam	39
A Red Herring	39
The Oracle of Love	39
Canine Cupidity	40
Fine and Dandy	41
The Battle Hymn of the Republic	41
Koan	41

Part III

Criminal Minds 45
The First Plateau 45
The Cobbler's Defense... 45
The First Litterbugs.. 46
Wow!... 47
The Creative Process... 47
Let's Blow this Joint!... 47
A Frugal Repast.. 48
Hola!.. 48
The Night Shift 48
The Flight of Fancy 49
Conviction.. 50
A Declaration of Sorts... 50
A-vowel 50
Redaction 51
A Grim Occupation 51
A Moral Compass 51
A Dangling Man... 52
5Embellishment 52
Population Explosion 52
"There's No There There."... 53
Infantilization... 53
The Power of Suggestion 53
The Prodigal... 54
C+... 54
A Chocolate Fetish 54
Murphy's Law 55
A Dismissive Missive 55
The Cuckoo Clock 55
Parlez-vous francais?... 56
The Best of Both Words 56
Beauty Fades.. 56
My Malibu Dream.. 57
Anchors Aweigh!.. 57
Horse Manure... 57
"Scorched Earth" 58
The Patriot Act 58
The Erroneous Zone.. 58
"Give Peace a Chance" 59

Part I

The Cat-and-Mouse Dichotomy

The cat and the mouse
Are quite a match.
The cat thinks the mouse
Is quite a catch.
The mouse thinks the cat
Should go away.
Then all the mice
Could come out and play.

Trying Times

When you fail to plan,
You plan to fail.
You might as well
Go straight to jail
And do the time
You deserve
And try again
When you get the nerve.

Labor Day

When a baby is born
A mother is made.
It's the dawn of the era
For which you have prayed
And the beginning of something
I can't explain
Except that it sometimes
Causes you pain.

Anatomy of a Teenager

I have ten fingers
And ten toes
Two arms and legs
And one big nose
I sing and dance
When I'm alone.
I think I
Must be a clone.

Justin Time

I waited a lonely lifetime
For my dream come true.
And when it finally happened
I got a room with a view.
Not even a doubting Thomas
Nor the denizen of the night
Could disabuse me of this feeling.
The timing was just right.

B.C. (Birth Canal)

A birthday is the sort of thing
No one should forget.
Everyone should post it
On the internet.
Indeed it is the sort of thing
Everyone should know
Until Father Time
Becomes your greatest foe.

Acrophobia

I would climb
The highest mountain
And sail the Seven Seas
And start my whole life over
If you would marry me.
I can't help but wonder
Just how far I'd go
Until I'd be torn asunder
Or get vertigo.

Adeste Fideles

Marriage is a proposal
I cannot accept.
You have been unfaithful
While the angels wept.
As much as you might like
To get a second chance
I must put an end
To our failed romance.

The Persistence of Memory

Hardly a day goes by
When I don't think of you,
The laughter and the love,
The good times we once knew.
That's now in the past.
The past is dead and gone.
But deep inside of me
The memory lives on.

When History Repeats Itself

It is what it is.
I am what I am.
You do what you do
As only you can.
Like it or not,
We fail to see
Life is just full
Of tautologies.

"La dolce vita"

Life is sweet
And, don't you know,
You see it
Everywhere you go.
But most of all
You see it when
The ice cream truck
Comes back again.

Mommy, Dearest

Theresa is alive and well
Living in our hearts.
Her virtue and nobility
Made her life an art.
We beatify and justify
But will she finally win
A place among the seraphim
When the saints go marching in?

Murder, She Wrote

It happened one Christmas
In the dead of night.
He was quite dead
And it was quite night.
The shot in the dark
Was heard by a few
But it happened so suddenly,
What could we do?

Word Power

Words are but the stepping stones
To better jobs and better homes;
To fancy cars and fancy wine;
To conversations when you dine;
Sometimes, I fear, I say too much
But I can't say this loud enough:
This I know because, like you,
I have them not but need them, too.

Future Perfect

I wish I could have known before
The way things were to be.
Then I would have done the things
I did differently.
There's really nothing to regret.
No one is to blame
For dashing all my hopes and dreams
And sullying my name.

The Elixir of Life

Everybody's doing it
And everybody knows
That when you are not doing it
You are in repose.
All you really need
Is one big, hairy nose
To fill your nasal passages
Before you decompose.

Aphrodite

They always painted Venus,
Venus and her mound,
Like a Vestal virgin
Above the madding crowd.
But we are so much wiser.
That's a load of crap.
To us she'll always be
An insatiable flytrap.

A Sober Thought

Step right up!
Life begins
After you
Admit your sins.
Clouds disperse.
Demons fade.
Now you're drinking
Lemonade!

"Placentam edeant!"*

She said it first.
(She was clever with words.)
Yet "Let them eat cake!"
Sounds so absurd.
Context is everything.
Context is key
To understanding history
And what makes us free.

*"Let them eat cake! (Latin)"

Keynesian Economics

I have the wisdom of Solomon
And the patience of Job
And a highly developed
Temporal lobe.
But the one thing I don't have,
I don't have a job.
And lately my prospects
Seem quite macabre.

No Pain, No Gain.

Welcome to my pity party.
Life is tragedy.
Anyone who lives,
Lives in misery.
Sadness leads to sorrow.
Sorrow leads to pain.
And pain leads to a threshold
We cannot explain.

"Et in Arcadia Ego"*

Elvis Presley lives today
If only in my heart.
I saw him only yesterday
At the Super Mart.
He looks the same as he once did.
He doesn't show his age
And shows no sign of digging in.
All the world's a stage.

*"Even in Arcadia (death)"

A Genteel Sufficiency

Poverty has been good to me.
"Genteel" is the word
Which means that I eat every day
But still am uninsured.
I have the bare necessities
One needs to get along
But a little bird inside my head
Tells me something's wrong.

Heart Strings

It's hard to say what went wrong
When you are in denial.
Your prickly skin will not allow you
One last fleeting smile.
I suppose it's just as well.
You never were that smart
When it came to handling
Affairs of the heart.

A Perfect Stranger

Tender is the night.
Tender is the day.
I met my one true love
Along life's narrow way.
We rhapsodize about
Love's long journey's end.
It was worth the wait.
On this you can depend.

A Boston Brahmin

Time has been a friend to me
Or so I am told.
I am all that I can be.
I'm as good as gold.
Modesty comes naturally.
I do the best I can
To lead a life of rectitude
And serve my fellowman.

Discretion is the Better Part of Valor

I'm given to hyperbole.
I exaggerate
For effect and oftentimes
To annihilate
My worthiest opponent
Or worst enemy
Who could not have known
I paid the referee.

A Veteran of Love

I have fought a million battles
And won a thousand wars
But my love for you
I cannot restore.
Once a love is lost
It cannot be found.
And this crazy world
Just keeps spinning 'round.

An Honest Man

You must be delirious
To think that I was serious
About my deleterious
Association with your friend.
Friends may come and friends may go.
I hate to say I told you so.
But I did and now you know
I will not pretend.

Levitations

I got what I wanted.
But was it worth the price?
Was it worth the price I paid
And the sacrifice?
It really doesn't matter.
When all is said and done,
I got what I wanted.
I had so much fun.

Gender Bias

I told the news reporter
Exactly what I'd seen.
He thanked me so profusely
You'd think I was the Queen.
I went home to listen
To the evening news.
He had his own agenda
Or he was confused.

Racial Bias

I told the news reporter
Exactly what I'd seen.
He thanked me so profusely
You'd think I was a King.
I went home to listen
To the evening news.
He had his own agenda
Or he was confused.

Unbiased

I was the news reporter.
It was exactly as I'd seen.
I thanked them so profusely.
You'd think I was James Dean.
I went home to listen
To the evening news.
I had my own agenda.
I should be recused.

"Honest Graft"

He was caught with his hand in the bucket.
His name was George Washington Plunkitt.
When in New York,
He ate lots of pork
And raped the municipal budget.

Strange Bedfellows

The bohemian and the bourgeois
Live side by side
In Greenwich Village
And the Lower East Side.
Only a knave
Would stop and stare
At the miscegenation
Of such a pair.

What's in a Name?

Harold was a Tease
And so was his son
And so was his son
If he ever had one.
I have often wondered
If he were more peeved
At being a herald
Or being a tease?

Caught in the Crosshairs

Sammy and Tabby
Don't need our permission
To realize
Their sole ambition
Vis-a-vis their predilection
To riddle each other
With contradictions.

The Smoking Gun

Oetzi, the Iceman,*
Who was found in the Alps,
Died of blunt force trauma
To the back of his scalp.
The blow was deadly.
The arrow was not.
The CAT scan determined
It was a rock.

*The 5,000-year-old mummy found frozen in the Italian Alps in 1991.

"Eye Popping Good"

Popcorn chicken.
Butterfly shrimp.
When it comes to catfish,
They don't skimp.
Mild or spicy.
We don't know why
We love that chicken
At Popeyes!

Part II

Sun to Sun

The world is full
Of windy bags,
Idle chatterers,
And useless nags.
I should know
Because I'm one.
A poet's work
Is never done.

The Hunting Party

Life's too short.
Don't you know
It's already
Time to go.
But before you do
Look around
At all the treasures
You have found.

The Antipode of Heaven

The time has come
To say goodbye
Although our love
Was just a lie,
A lie we lived
All too well,
A lie that was
A living hell.

Catnip

We have one kitty
And one cat.
Sam is good
But Tab's a brat.
We love them both
Just the same
Although they drive us
Both insane.

Ambrose Bierce

Cynicism comes easily
When all else has failed.
A cynic is the kind of man
Who knows his shipped has sailed.
Sincerity is the first to go
Followed by old friends
Who do not know why it is
You misapprehend.

Fantasy Island

The dreams I dreamed
Have all come true.
The dreams I dreamed
Were all of you.
The dreams I dreamed
Are alive and well
For how long
Only time will tell.

Deaf Ears

Listen is the one thing
A kitten cannot do.
He hears just fine
But hasn't got a clue
That what you are saying
Pertains to him.
Any hope of improvement
Is really quite slim.

Genetic Determinism

I hold myself responsible
For the things you have done.
I am your father
And you are my son.
The sins of the father
Are visited upon
All hapless offspring
At conception.

Proceed at Your Own Peril

To put the past behind you
Is the hardest thing to do.
To put your best foot forward
And embrace that which is new
Takes more courage than rote learning.
You must come to see
That you are judged by what you do.
That is history.

Plunder

I was caught in flagrante delicto
By the CEO
Embezzling funds
From a rodeo show.
The moral of this tale
(If there is one)
Is stick to your story
Attila the Hun.

Wordplay

Lima is a bean.
Brussel is a sprout.
We all come from somewhere.
Figure it out.
Scotch is a whiskey.
Burgundy is a wine.
They only get harder
And more defined.

Cognitive Dissonance

We hate to learn
And learn to hate.
There's not much
To celebrate
In our lives
Of desperation
With our vain
Expectation.

Smoke Screen

I was watching you watching me
Sitting at the bar.
I was quite surprised that you were
Smoking a cigar.
You had quit cold turkey
Many years ago.
It wouldn't hurt to try the patch
My admiring Romeo.

Screw the Middleman

Every fait accompli
Is also a done deed.
You get what you want.
Or you get what you need.
Heaven is above us.
Hell is down below.
We are in between
Playing tick-tack-toe.

Black Death

The two things in life
I avoid like the Hague
Are the AIDS pandemic
And the bubonic plague.
We know in our hearts,
We know deep inside
That, when it comes to death,
There is no place to hide.

Que sera, sera!

We can never know
What is to be,
Where we are going,
What we will see.
But we can always know
Where we have been
Recycling our mistakes
Again and again.

Heat Wave

I was born in April
But conceived in July.
I can't begin to tell you
When or where or why
Except to say that in July,
More often than not,
The temperature in Chicago
Gets really, really hot.

A Half Truth

"Each day is a new beginning
When you're young at heart."
I read that in the window
Of the mini mart.
I only half believe it
Because it is half true.
Each day is a new beginning
Because I'm here with you.

Greco-Roman Decadence

Sybaris was a place of joy
Where every little girl and boy
Did their best in every way
To reverse the signs of moral decay.
While love is found most everywhere,
(Who does not have love to share?)
The search for love was there the rage
According to a Delphic sage.

A Police Intervention

I went out to smoke a beer
And drink a cigarette.
I knew this was my lucky day,
So, I placed a bet.
"Why is that ball spinning
Above the red and black?"
I asked the man arresting me,
"I thought this was Blackjack!"

"A Wanton Disregard"

Everything I want
And everything I need
Are one and the same.
(The Nicene Creed)
But I believe that some things
Are better left unsaid
Like what we say and do
When we go bed.

Eternity

"Every day's a new day,"
Is a common refrain.
Every day's a construct
Deep inside our brain.
Every day's a fortnight
Every week or two.
Every day's a lifetime
When I'm here with you.

Sanctuary

Some people find great solace
In the bosom of the Church.
Other people find real comfort
In the swaying of a birch.
I prefer the birch myself
Because it is so strong
Although the history of the Church
Is so very long.

Disillusionment

In this land of broken dreams
And unmitigated sorrow
We get by with just our wits
And hang on for tomorrow.
Therapy may be an option
But it may be too late
To heal those wounds of disaffection
That turns bitterness to hate.

Greek Freak

I believe in miracles.
I believe in fate.
I don't believe in anything
That does not levitate.
Gravity just brings you down.
God knows that's the truth.
Sophistry will always be
The error of my youth.

Spiritual Cremation

You have made my life complete.
You have made me smile.
You have made my dreams come true
And my life worthwhile.
You're my singularity
And my heart's desire.
You are everything to me.
You set my soul on fire.

Triage

When I get up in the morning
The first thing I do
Is feed my little kitties
And have a drink or two.
The last thing I remember
Before I close my eyes
Is how much I get done
When I prioritize.

Voyeurism

Ships are passing
In the night.
. There's not another
Soul in sight.
The night is young
And so are we.
They sit home
And watch TV.

Bibliomania

A classic is the kind of book
That you have to read.
A mystery is the kind of book
About a dreadful deed.
A romance is the kind of book
That you love to love.
A thriller is the kind of book
That's all of the above.

Glasnost

East is east and west is west.
The two shall never meet.
But if they do I say to you
It will spell defeat
For the power whose final hour
Will then come to pass
As foretold in days of old
By Balaam's ass.

V-J Day

Truman gave the order
For the Enola Gay to fly
Which caused the deaths
Of many samurai
But saved the lives
Of countless GI's
Although I admit
I oversimplify.

"Fraternite"

The Statue of Liberty
Is the beacon of hope
That welcomed the masses
And helped them elope.
This icon of freedom
Was a gift from the French
Who thought that our friendship
Should be more entrenched.

Flotsam and Jetsam

Clutter, clutter, everywhere
Fills my life with dark despair.
Clutter, clutter in my home.
I'm afraid to sleep alone.
Cutter, clutter, mother-lode.
In my dreams how you explode.
Clutter, clutter is alright
Once you learn to expedite.

A Red Herring

Only the daring and slightly uncaring
Would lead you off the trail.
But when they do, don't feel blue.
It's only a minor detail.
Every whodunit or newspaper pundit
Will fool you if you if he can
To spruce up his story and win for him glory.
He had the nicest tan.

The Oracle of Love

Hurry! The clock is ticking.
Ticking all the time.
We don't have much longer
To decide what's yours and mine.
Who knew this would happen?
Who knew there'd come a day
When you and I would fall apart
And go our separate ways?

Canine Cupidity

We had a German Shepherd
Living in our yard.
She was totally smitten
With a Saint Bernard.
I did my best to warn her
It was a mistake.
Alas, she would not listen.
She loved the shiftless rake.

Fine and Dandy

I love my little binke.
His name is Pink Pierre.
Whenever I need comfort,
He is always there.
We play every morning
Beneath the old oak tree
Deep inside the forest
In my reverie.

The Battle Hymn of the Republic*

The righteous are always right.
They will tell you so.
The damned are always damned
Ex officio.
But only a chosen few,
Who know right from wrong,
Can set those words to music
In a sacred song.

*Homage to Julia Ward Howe

Koan

The heart has its reasons.
Time has its seasons.
I have you and you have me.
What else could there possibly be?

Part III

Criminal Minds

Give me opportunity.
Find me a job.
I'd be amenable
To joining the mob.
Spare me the indignity
Of waiting in line.
Spare me the temptation
Of the perfect crime.

The First Plateau

It matters not that you can't speak
And never get enough to eat.
It matters not that you aren't funny
(You get more flies with honey).
It matters not that you take umbrage.
To anybody wearing plumage.
What matters is you can wait.
You still have another eight.

The Cobbler's Defense

I took the Fifth Amendment
To spare you any pain.
And if I could you know I would
Do it all again.
To empathize with someone
Is to wear his shoes.
They made me an offer
I couldn't refuse.

The First Litterbugs

Hansel and Gretel
Made it O.K.
To leave all your crap
And be on your way.
One man's detritus
Is another man's flan.
All you can do is
Catch-as-catch-can.

Wow!

Onomatopoeia
Is all the rage
In the boardroom
And on the stage.
I don't understand
What the buzz is about.
We just moan and groan.
You figure it out.

The Creative Process

When I fall victim
To writer's block,
I go the phone
And dial a lot.
Then I hang up
And start writing again
And hope that I'm able
To produce a gem.

Let's Blow This Joint!

I'm so sorry if I let you down
But you were very high
On the stuff your mother told you
You should never try.
Mary Jane has no ambition.
Look into her eyes.
The price of drug addiction
Is always super-sized.

A Frugal Repast

I took a correspondence course
At the local "Y."
It really made me wonder
If I could really try
To write a book of poetry
And be so debonair
Or stick with what I'm doing now—
That's eating three meals square.

Hola!

It was a tempest in a Teapot Dome
Of the highest order.
"I-am-not-a-crook,"
He told the tape recorder.
But that is nothing when compared
To the grave disorder
That currently exists
On our national border.

The Night Shift

I used to be a beggar
But now I am a thief.
It pays a little better
But I get more grief.
And then, I have to tell you,
A thief must work at night.
Only home invasions
Are done in broad daylight.

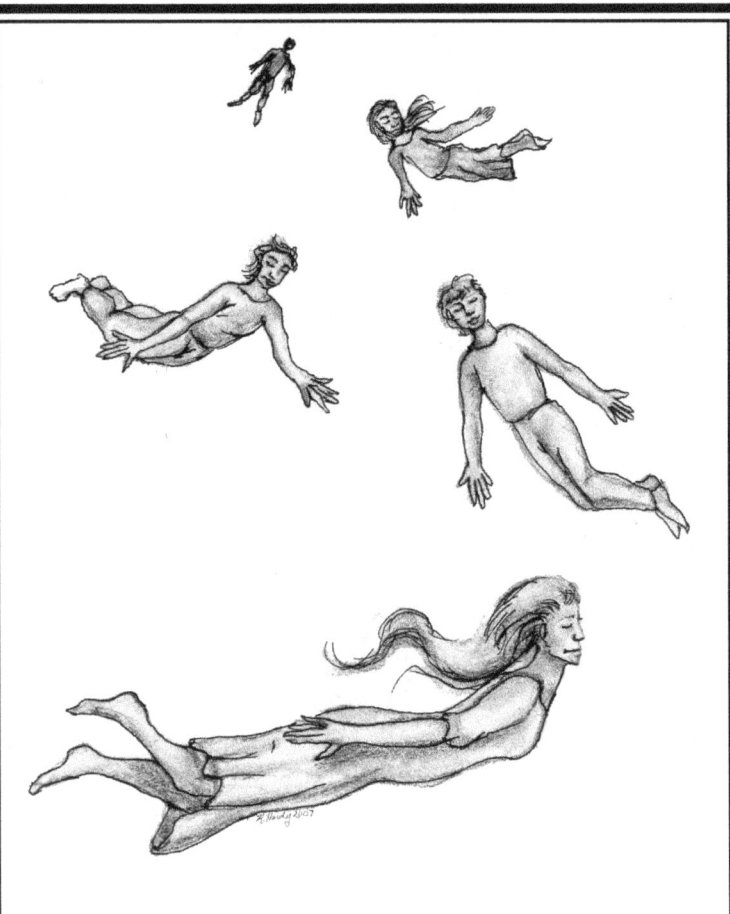

The Flight of Fancy

I fly by night. I fly by day.
It's the only way.
If you could fly, would you stay
On this big runway?
There are those who do oppose
The higher altitudes.
You must gain their deepest trust
To earn more latitude.

Conviction

I took a vow of poverty.
It's going pretty well.
There isn't much to do here
Living in this cell.
Sometimes I want to break these chains
And start my life anew.
But instead I am a mendicant
Waiting for my stew.

A Declaration of Sorts

You took my money.
You took my time.
You got yours.
Now I'll get mine.
All is fair in
Love and war.
I have heard
It all before.

A-vowel

A diphthong and an umlaut
Function differently.
One combines sounds
And the other discretely
Divides them up like silver
Put out for sale.
Are we a U.S.
Or are we the grail?

Redaction

I can be a "supernova"
Only in my dreams.
But that's better than nothing
Strange as it seems.
When it comes to writing,
Editing is key.
No one knows this better
Than little 'ole me.

A Grim Occupation

I live my life graciously
On the primrose path.
I see what I want to see
Or its aftermath.
The future looks so good to me
I often wonder why
When we have so much to do
We still have time to die.

A Moral Compass

It takes a long, long time
To get from here to there.
It takes a heavy toll
In normal wear and tear.
No matter what you do
Always take a map
To tell you where to go
And to avoid the obvious traps.

A Dangling Man

"I won't tell you where I'm going to be at
Because you already know."
"I don't remember what he spoke about.
That was so long ago."
I will verbally chastise
Any unwitting fool
Who dangles his participles
And thinks that it is cool.

Embellishment

From St. Peter's to St. Petersburg
I have seen it all.
And, I must confess,
I have had a ball.
But the one thing I cannot abide
In my waking dream
Is the person who tries to make things
Better than they seem.

Population Explosion

If you believe them,
You'd think all this storming
Is nothing short
Of global warming.
What's wrong with this picture?
Incredulously,
The world's always been
As hot as can be.

"There's No There There."

I took it under advisement
Not to fall in love.
This was celebrated
In the stars above.
But there's one small problem
With my newfound bliss.
When I go to bed,
There's no one there to kiss.

Infantilization

I have been the victim of
A psycobable state.
They promised to release me
But I think it's too late.
Dependence is a condition
I dare not forsake.
To start over now
Would be a big mistake.

The Power of Suggestion

It was a real coincidence
I met you at that bar,
Shopping at the grocery store,
Standing by your car.
Of course, that global positioning system
Wasn't my idea
But I bought it anyway,
Momma, Momma Mia!

The Prodigal

I have to say that just today
I took Holy Communion.
I smiled a lot and soon forgot
This was a spiritual reunion.
Religious theory makes me weary
Of fundamentalist rant.
And the call of the wild makes this child
Only want to recant.

C+

I must confess, under duress,
The wisdom of your logic
Is so sublime but unrefined.
It is pedagogic.
Few can know your personal woe
In arriving at a scheme.
But I can tell you went through hell
Developing this theme.

A Chocolate Fetish

I drove to the grocery store
To buy a Snickers bar.
I ate it at the service desk
And then went to my car.
I loitered in the parking lot
For more than an hour
Watching the bagger swagger
Like a superpower.

Murphy's Law

The facts are in evidence.
The evidence is in.
Witness protection
Is about to kick in.
What's wrong with this picture?
I hate to think
That, in the heat of the argument,
I just might blink.

A Dismissive Missive

I took it upon myself
To write you this note
From which I warn you
I liberally quote.
It says "I love you"
But (I paraphrase)
It's just that I'm going
Through a terrible phase.

The Cuckoo Clock

A cuckoo flew over
The International Date Line
Only to find himself
In another time.
"Well, I'll be," he said
Under his breath,
"This is much better
Than faking my death."

Parlez-vous francais?

Only a fashionista
Could confirm that it is true
When father met our mother
She wore stockings made of blue.
A "bluestocking" is a woman
(All pedantry aside),
Who loves to read and write
About the Treaty of Versailles.

The Best of Both Words

The belligerent and the bellicose
Send us off to war.
But the peaceful and pacific
Are who we adore.
Why not take the four
And make from them two words?
"Bellipeace" and "pacificose"
Make "hawk and dove" lovebirds.

Beauty Fades

I went to the Seapearl,
A trendy oyster bar,
And met someone special
Gazing from afar.
He offered me a drink,
Which I gladly took,
But I didn't like him
After a closer look.

My Malibu Dream

If wishes were horses
And dreams could come true
I'd ride to the ocean
To be with you.
I know it sounds funny
But that's where you'd be
Sitting there patiently
Waiting for me.

Anchors Aweigh!

There comes a time in each man's life
When he must go away.
There comes a time in each man's life
When he must stay away.
There comes a time in each man's life
When he must find a way.
There comes a time in each man's life…
I think today's the day.

Horse Manure

History would be different
In inexplicable ways
If the Greeks had left ten gift cards
In a ceramic vase.
The Trojans could have used them
At any Target Store
And surely would have gone on
To win that crazy war.

"Scorched Earth"

You are morally responsible
For getting in that fight.
I haven't told your father
But I think that I just might
Just to teach you a lesson
You should have already learned:
When you play with fire
You will always get burned.

The Patriot Act

It used to be a civic duty
To conduct a citizen's arrest
When domestic tranquility
Was put to the test.
Now every facet of our polity
Must remain secured
If random acts of violence
Are to be deterred.

The Erroneous Zone

I exited my comfort zone
A long time ago
And now write about things
I don't really know
Which creates for me a challenge
I can't always meet
The result of which is something
I dare not repeat.

"Give Peace a Chance"

He entered old Jerusalem
On a donkey's back.
When it came to free publicity
They say he had a knack.
We celebrate the miracle
Of his Virgin birth.
All he ever wanted
Was to establish peace on earth.

www.ingramcontent.com/pod-product-compliance
Lightning Source LLC
Chambersburg PA
CBHW031216090426
42736CB00009B/940